All About Food Crops

CORN

Cecelia H. Brannon

Enslow Publishing
101 W. 23rd Street
Suite 240
New York, NY 10011
USA
enslow.com

Published in 2018 by Enslow Publishing, LLC
101 W. 23rd Street, Suite 240, New York, NY 10011

Library of Congress Cataloging-in-Publication Data

Names: Brannon, Cecelia H., author. | Brannon, Cecelia H. All about food crops.
Title: Corn / Cecelia H. Brannon.
Description: New York, NY : Enslow Publishing, 2018. | Series: All about food crops | Audience: Pre-K to grade 1. | Includes bibliographical references and index.
Identifiers: LCCN 2017002021| ISBN 9780766085794 (library-bound) | ISBN 9780766088245 (pbk.) | ISBN 9780766088184 (6-pack)
Subjects: LCSH: Corn—Juvenile literature.
Classification: LCC SB191.M2 B7175 2018 | DDC 633.1/5—dc23
LC record available at https://lccn.loc.gov/2017002021

Printed in the United States of America

To Our Readers: We have done our best to make sure all websites in this book were active and appropriate when we went to press. However, the author and the publisher have no control over and assume no liability for the material available on those websites or on any websites they may link to. Any comments or suggestions can be sent by email to customerservice@enslow.com.

Photo Credits: Cover, p. 1 Peter Kim/Shutterstock.com; pp. 3 (left), 8 Ken Felepchuk/Shutterstock .com; pp. 3 (center), 6 Vadym Zaitsev/Shutterstock.com; pp. 3 (right), 10 Susan Montgomery/ Shutterstock.com; pp. 4–5 MNBB Studio/Shutterstock.com; p. 12 napocska/Shutterstock.com; p. 14 BLACKDAY/Shutterstock.com; p. 16 Ildi Papp/Shutterstock.com; p. 18 minadezhda/Shutterstock.com; p. 20 Mariyana M/Shutterstock.com; p. 22 Elena Schweitzer/Shutterstock.com.

Contents

Words to Know

bushels

kernels

maze

Corn is an important crop.

The little yellow parts we eat are called kernels. The green, leafy outside part is called the husk.

Corn is grown in a large field. The amount of corn grown is measured in bushels.

After the corn has been picked, many people make mazes out of the stalks. Corn mazes are fun to walk through!

Corn is a popular food for people and animals. Farmers often feed corn to their chickens.

But corn is not just for eating. It is turned into a special chemical used to make fuel.

Corn can also be ground into cornmeal. This is used to make many different foods, such as tortillas and corn bread.

When cornmeal is ground more, it makes cornstarch. Cornstarch is used to make foods like sauces and soups thick.

Corn can be cooked down into a syrup. This is often used to sweeten things, such as sodas and desserts.

Corn is both delicious and useful!

Read More

Borth, Teddy. *Crops on the Farm*. North Mankato, MN: Capstone Classroom, 2016.

Nelson, Robin. *From Kernel to Corn*. Minneapolis, MN: Lerner Publications, 2012.

Rattini, Kristin Baird. *National Geographic Readers: Seed to Plant*. Washington, DC: National Geographic, 2014.

Websites

Science for Kids
www.scienceforkidsclub.com/plant-lifecycle.html
Read about how plants grow.

Science Kids
www.sciencekids.co.nz/sciencefacts/food/corn.html
Learn more facts about corn.

Index

Guided Reading Level: B
Guided Reading Leveling System is based on the guidelines recommended by Fountas and Pinnell.

Word Count: 160